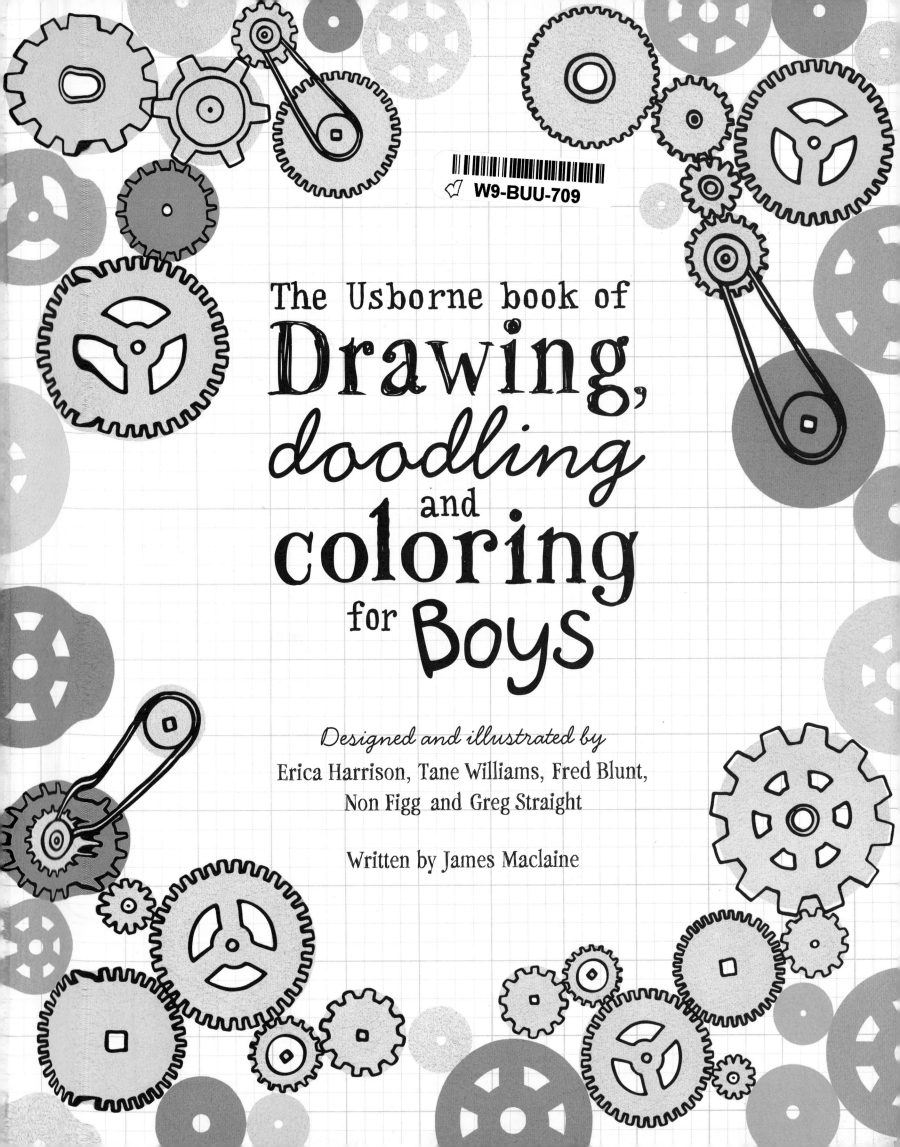

The Usborne book of Drawing, doodling and coloring for Boys

Designed and illustrated by
Erica Harrison, Tane Williams, Fred Blunt,
Non Figg and Greg Straight

Written by James Maclaine

How to use this book...

On some of the pages you'll find ideas for what to do, but you can do whatever you like.

Use pens, pencils or crayons to complete the pictures.

You could fill in large areas, or add stripes, spots or patterns of your own.

When you draw on top of a shape with a pen, wait for a couple of seconds for the ink to dry, so that it doesn't smudge.

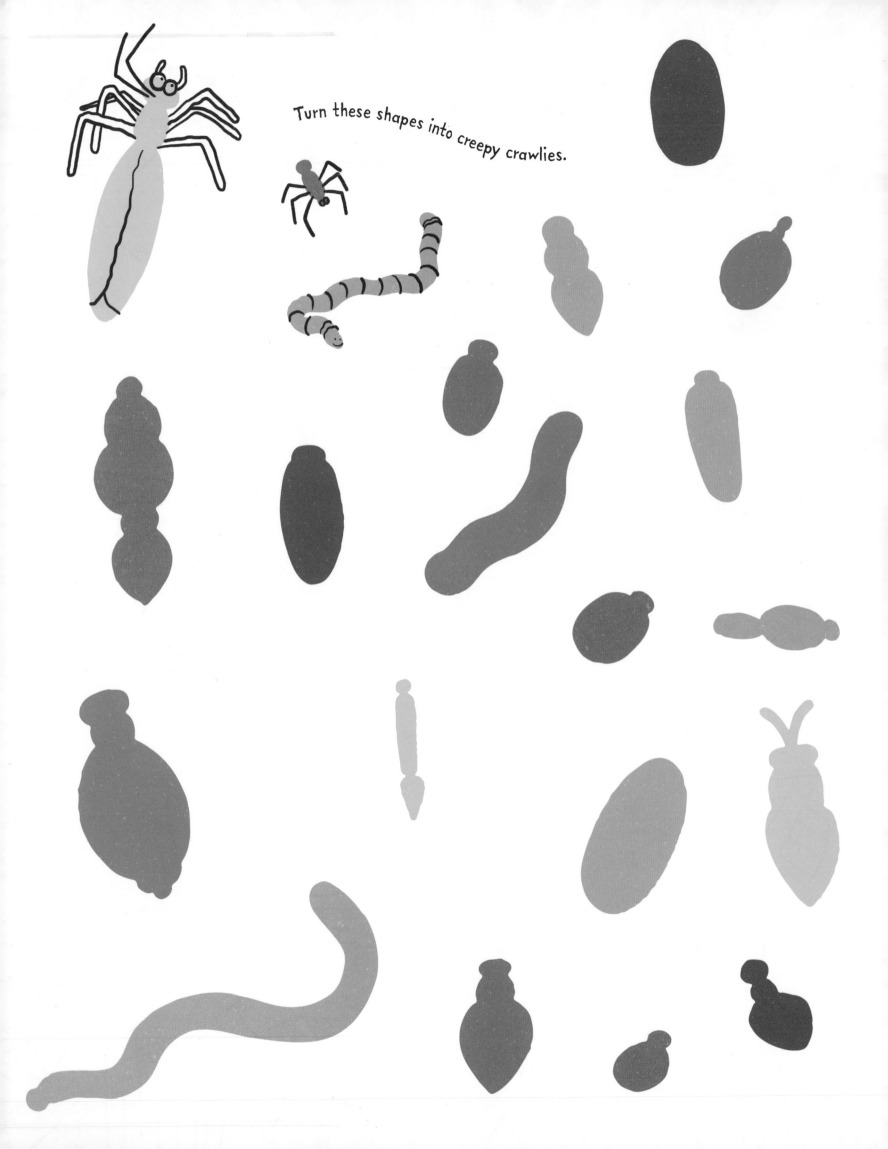

Turn these shapes into creepy crawlies.

Add eyes, wings, legs and antennae.

Draw in the missing faces. Can you completely fill the pages with ghosts?

Whoooo

Ooo

Boo

Doodle patterns on
these bicycles with
a black pen.

Using the triangles as a guide, take lines for a walk across this page...

...and down this side.

Turn these shapes into cogs.

Connect some with belts, too.

Add black birds perching on the branches and wires.

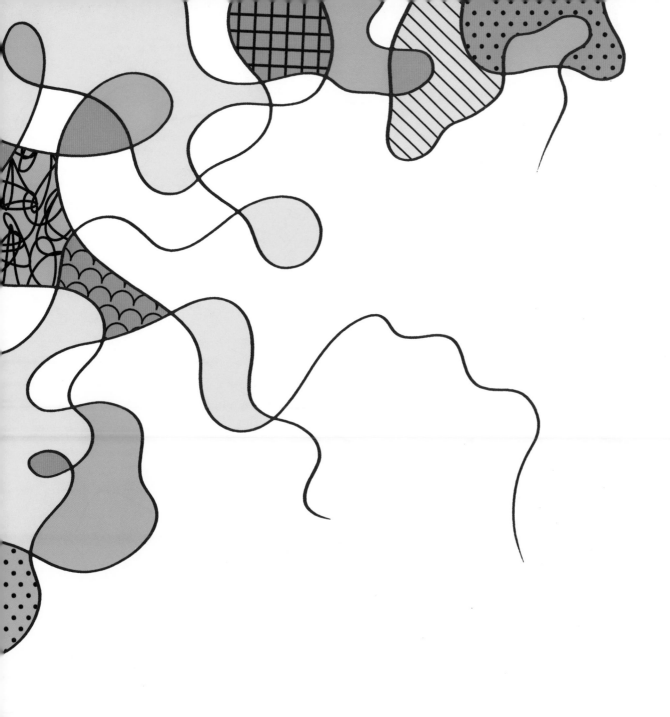

Fill the page with overlapping squiggly lines and patterns.

Design different outfits for these superheroes.

Doodle a hairy-legged spider dangling from each thread.

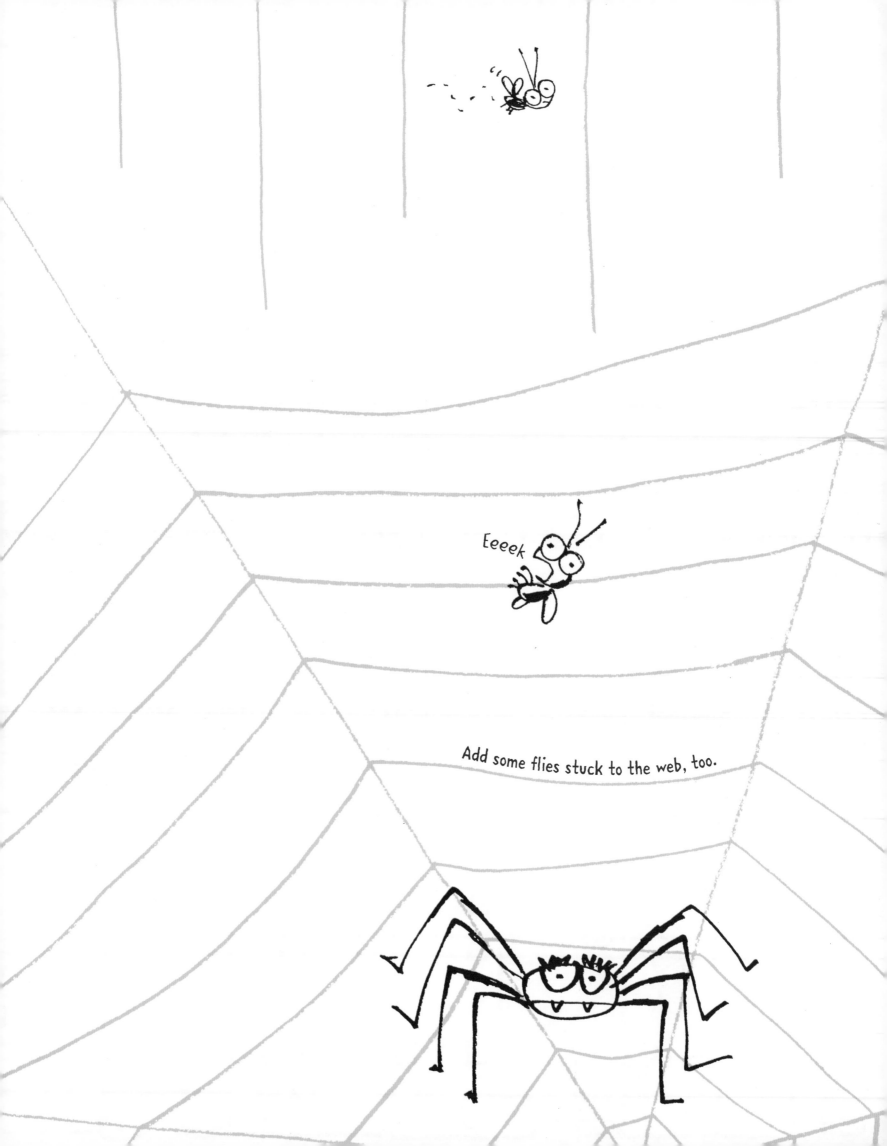

Eeeek

Add some flies stuck to the web, too.

Choose lots of felt-tip pens
to finish these robots.

Draw long-tongued frogs and hovering flies.

slurp!

Fill these winding roads with cars and trucks.

Scribble on the clouds and write in the speech bubbles, too.

Draw some whales and
doodle lots of waves.

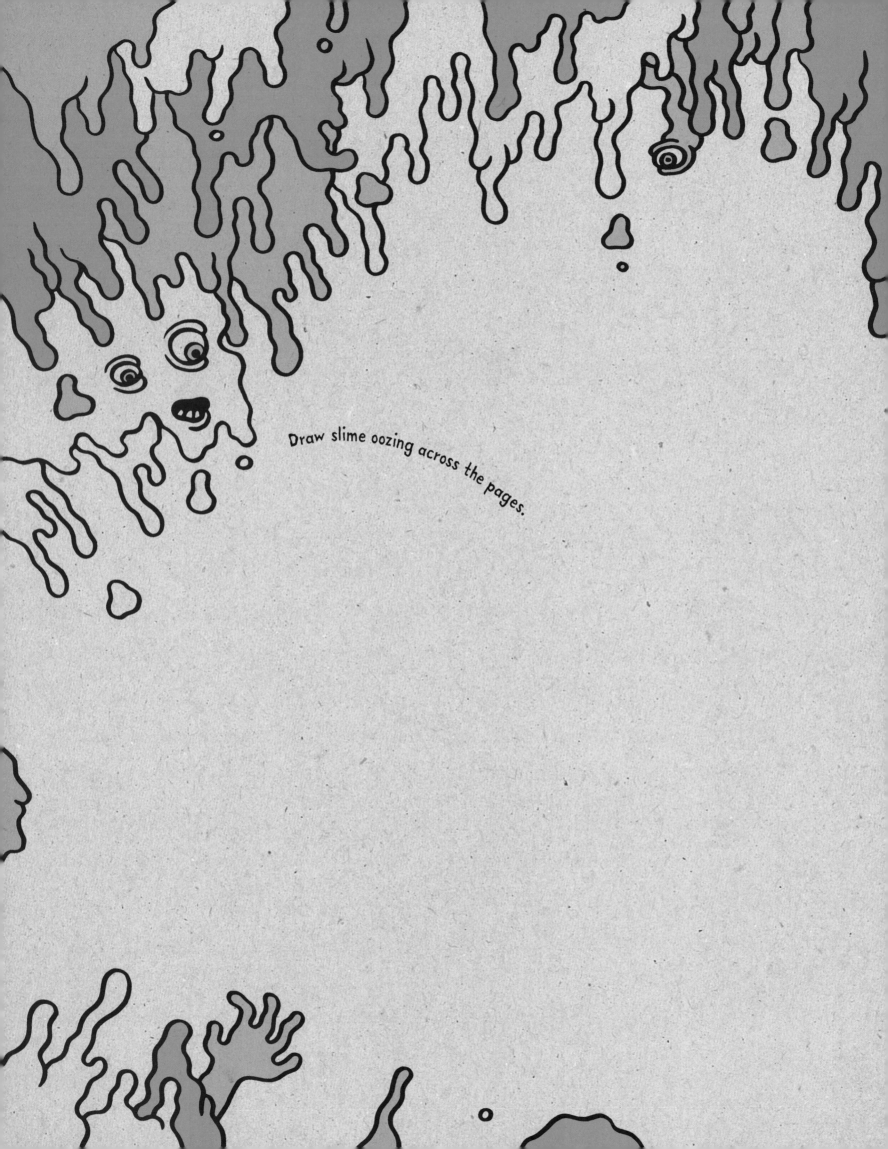

Draw slime oozing across the pages.

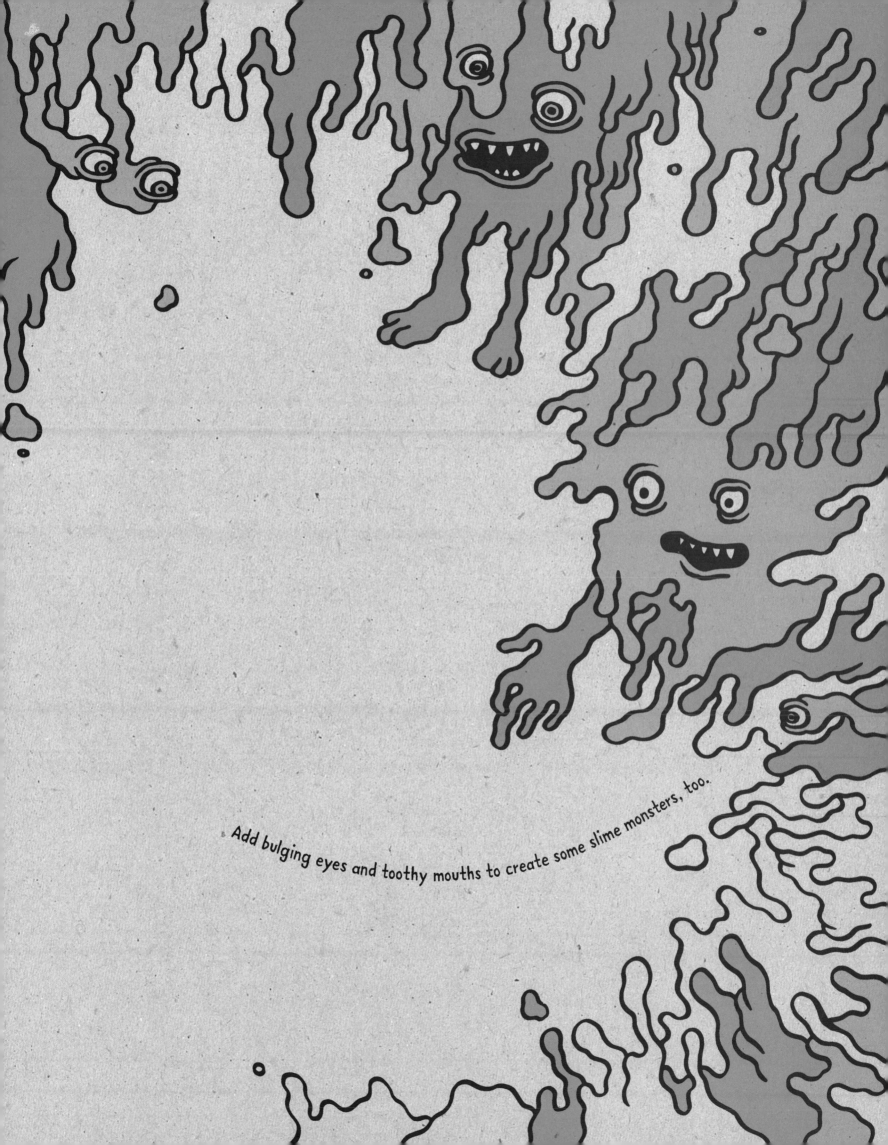

Add bulging eyes and toothy mouths to create some slime monsters, too.

Turn these shapes into fire-breathing dragons.

Add lots of scales, horns and scary teeth.

Complete the skyscrapers and doodle lots more.

Finish the rows of monster trucks.

Vroom, vroom, vroom...

Add some bumps for them to drive over.

Doodle disguises.

Draw faces in the empty frames, too.

Draw sea creatures frightened by
the giant octopus...

oo err

...and doodle suckers on its tentacles.

Keep doodling triangles, patterns and trucks until you can doodle no more.

Continue this
camouflage pattern.

Turn these fingerprints into different faces.

Happy...

...sleepy...

...angry...

...or scared?

Draw different warships to make this battle even bigger.

Doodle action stickmen...

...fighting...

...swimming...

...kicking...

...or climbing.

Turn these shapes into tigers with stripes, claws and teeth.

GRRr

Add scribbly manes to these lions, too.

ROARR

RAA

Draw strange-looking sea creatures lurking at the bottom of the sea.

Add ghosts, monsters and ladders to the different levels.

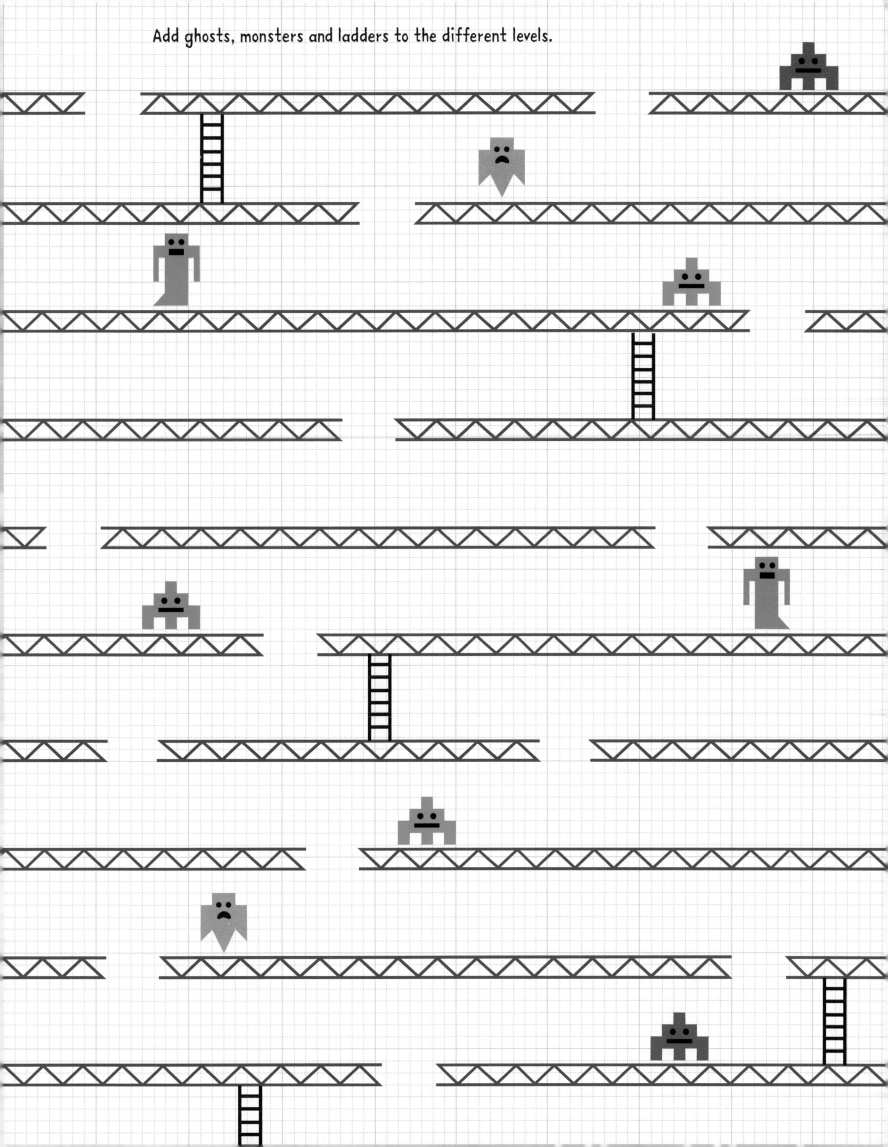

Turn the shapes into monsters attacking a city.
Then, doodle vehicles and people fighting back.

BOOM...

Draw ladders,
steps, ropes, and
stickmen, too.

Connect the science equipment with tubes to finish the picture.

fizz

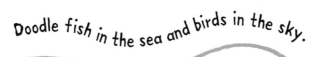

Doodle fish in the sea and birds in the sky.

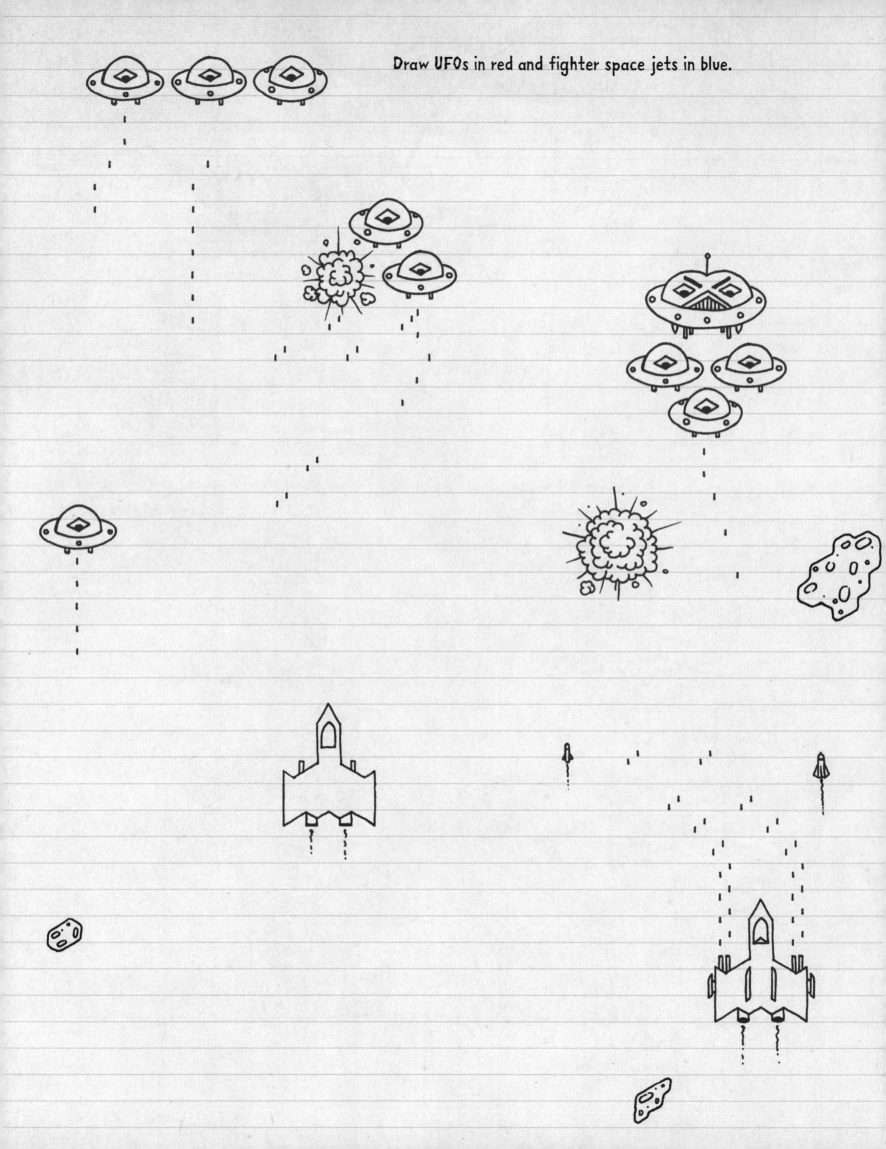

Draw **UFOs** in red and fighter space jets in blue.

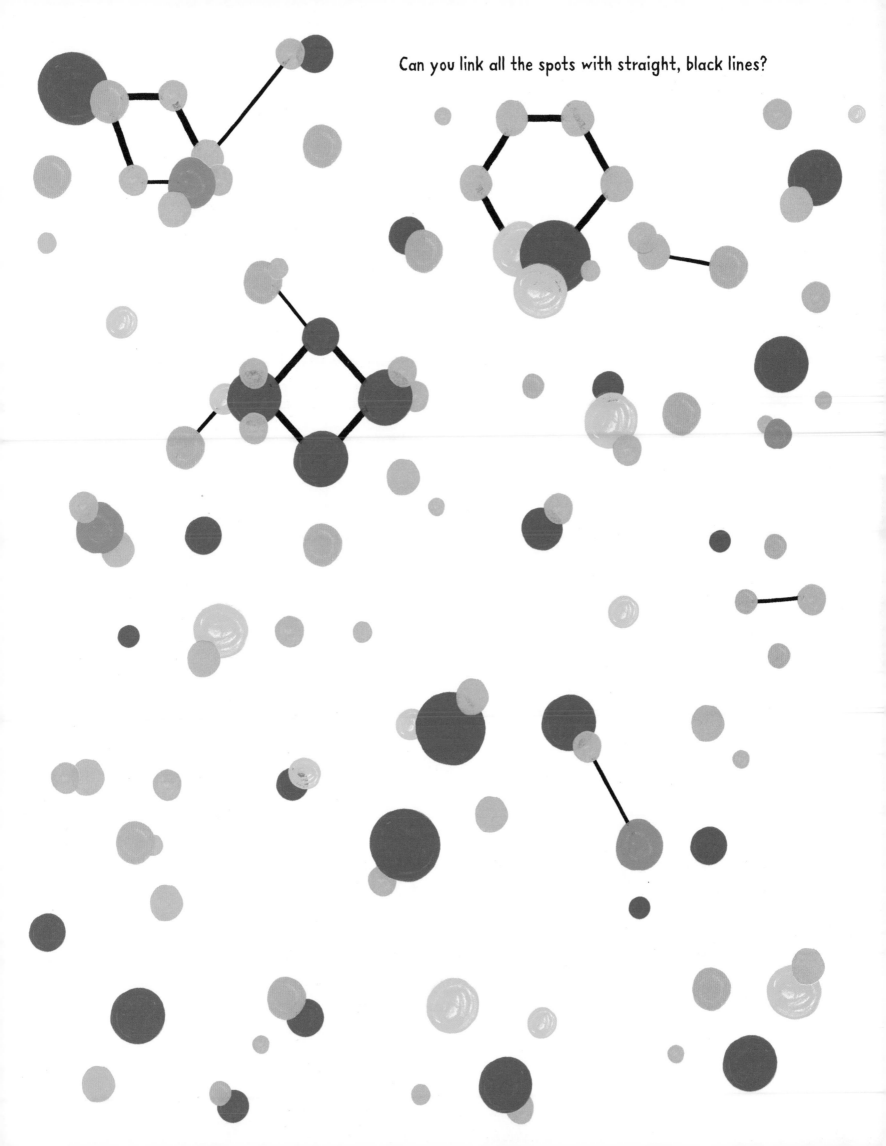

Can you link all the spots with straight, black lines?

ta-da

Give these strongmen weights to lift.

Add faces to the crowd.

Doodle patterns on
their leotards, too.

ugggh

Use every pen and pencil
you have to fill in the
triangle monsters.

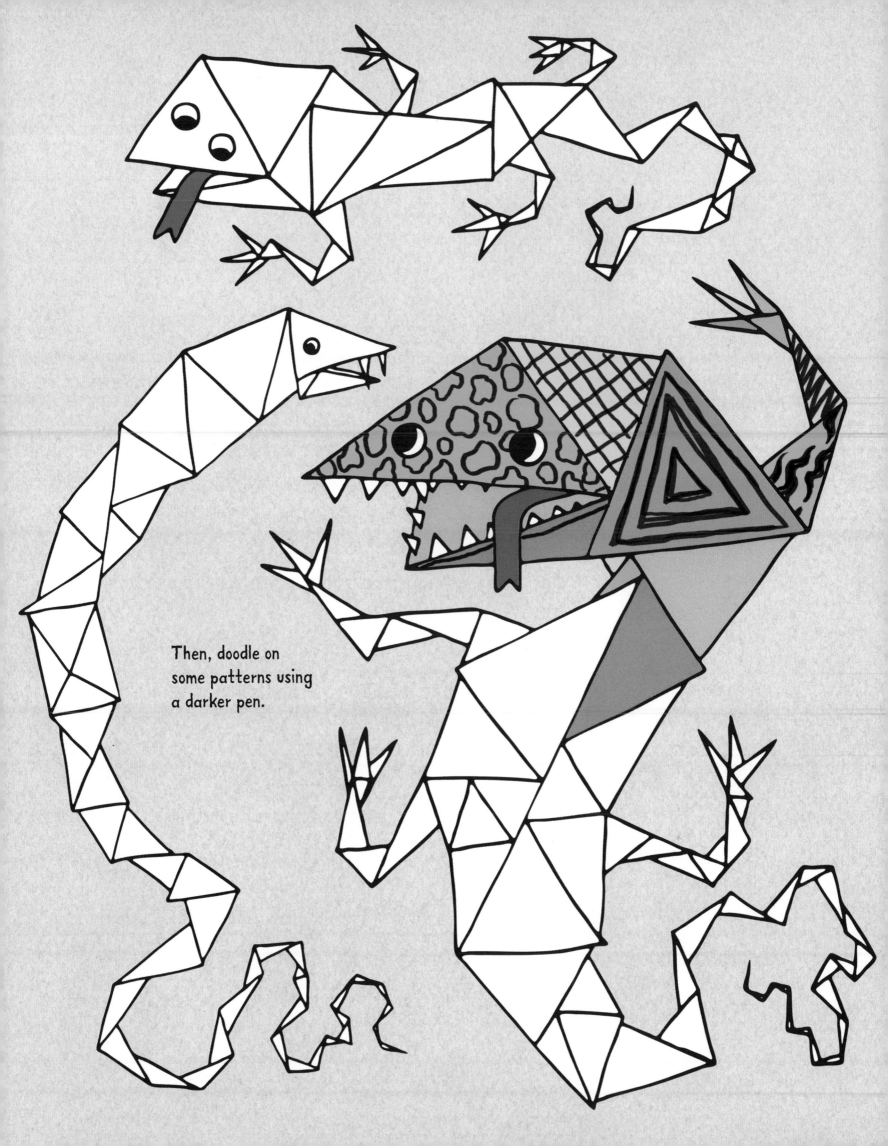

Then, doodle on
some patterns using
a darker pen.

Design the figures' clothes.

Turn each spot into a different face.

Hello

My name's Monty

Maybe add hair, a bow tie or a hat?

Doodle angry faces on the clouds and raindrops.

BOOM

Yo, ho, ho, ho, ho...
Finish these pirates.

Add hooks, cutlasses, boots...

...and speech bubbles.

Doodle lots of treasure, too.

Fill in this crazy machine.

Draw an alien inside each flying saucer.

Fill in the snakes with different patterns.

HISSSS

HISS

Draw your own snakes
on this page.

Turn each shape into a different person.

Doodle faces and bodies on these numbers...

3 0 0 1 6

9 7 4

5 1 3 8

8 4 2

7 0 5

x g b p

t u s

i f e r

d y w

You called?

h k c z

Can you complete the circuit board? Add circles, squares and lines, and any other shapes you like.

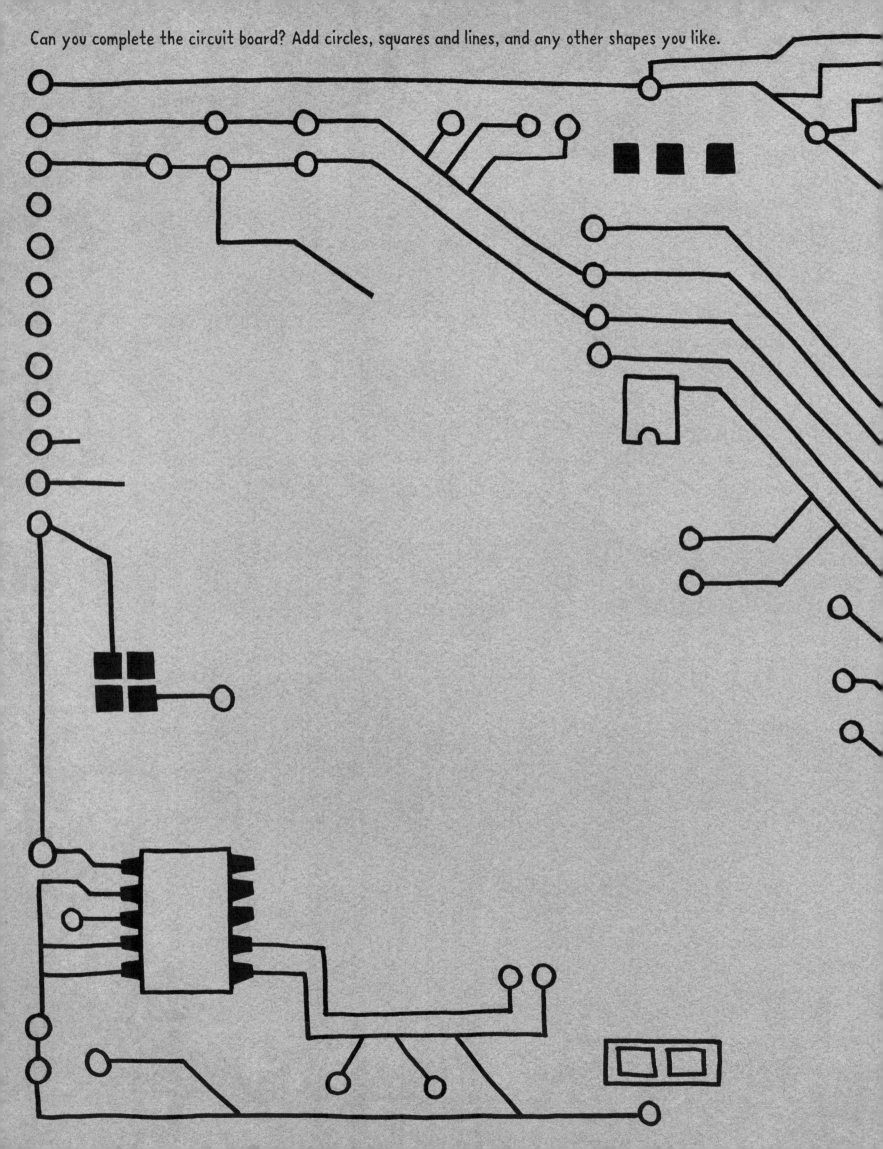

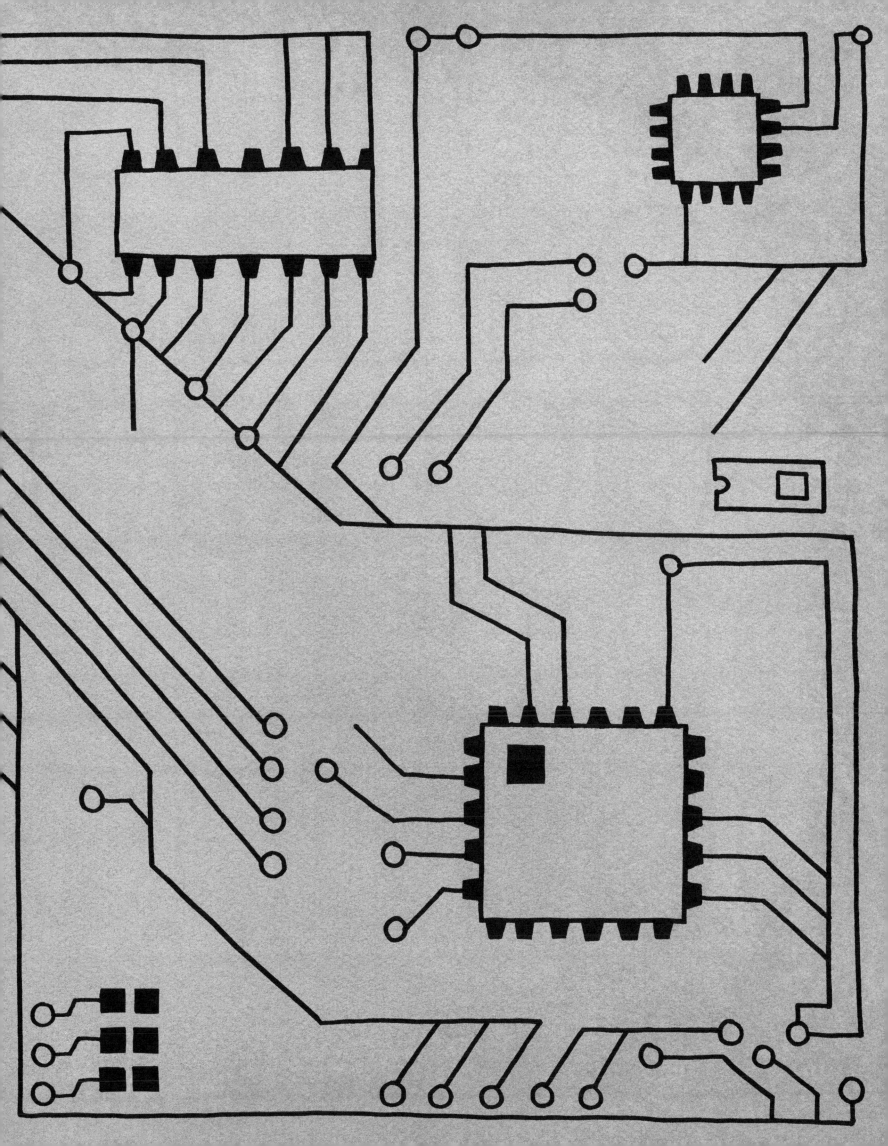

Decorate
the masks.

Continue this pattern without
taking your pen off the paper.

Customize the boots and shoes with your own patterns.

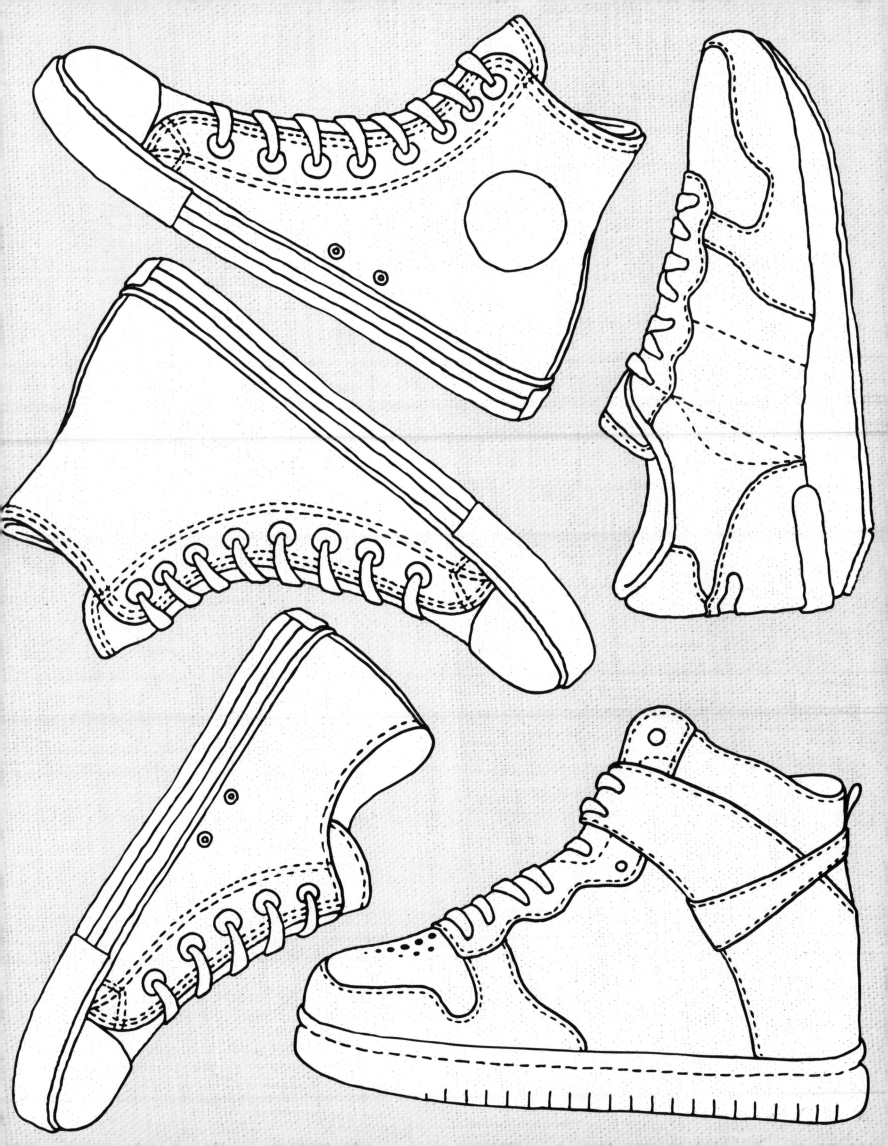

Turn these shapes into eyeballs.

Draw bats flying in the sky and hanging from the trees.

Fill these boxes with whatever you like.

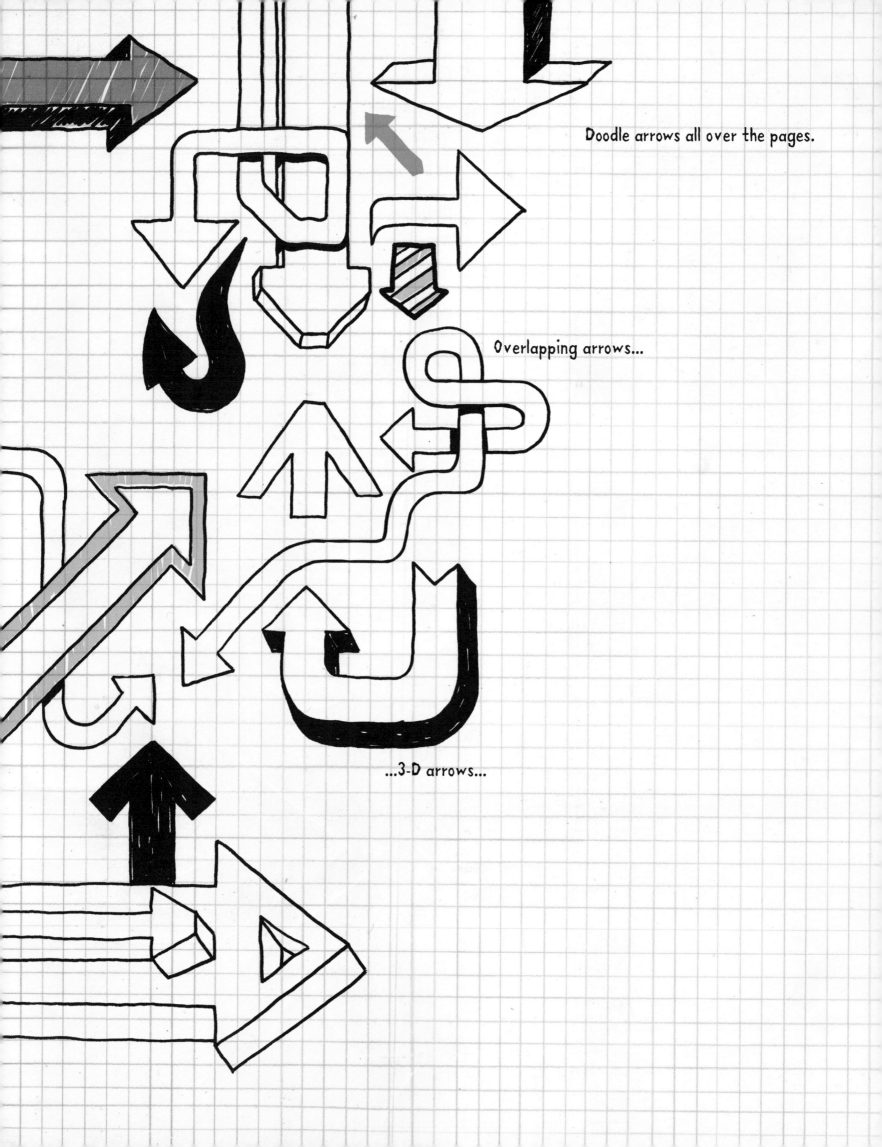

Doodle arrows all over the pages.

Overlapping arrows...

...3-D arrows...

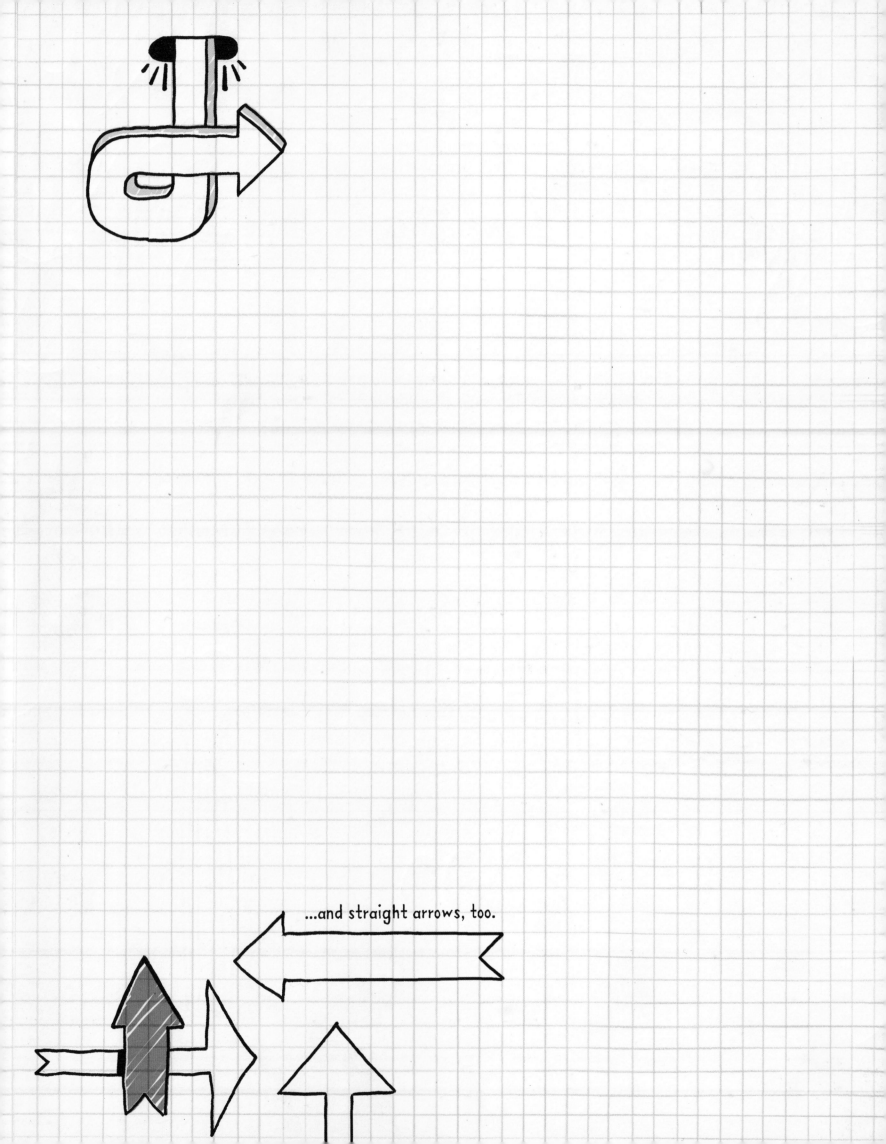

...and straight arrows, too.

When in Rome, doodle as the Romans do.

Turn the shapes into arches...

...columns...

...and temples, too.

Finish these rows of patterns before doodling some more.

whirr...

...CLANG!

Give the robots eyes,
teeth, legs and arms.

Doodle dials, buttons and lights on their bodies.

Create a city.

Using the triangles as a guide,
doodle sea monsters and waves.

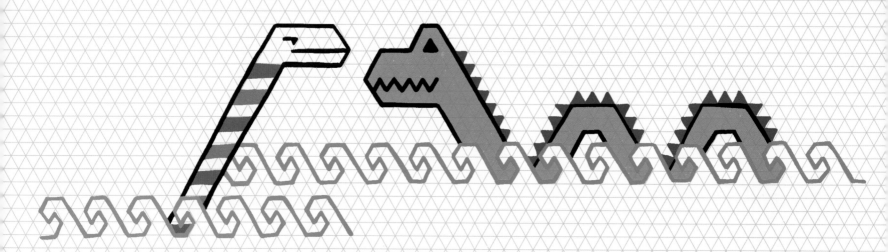

Fill the page with a pattern of shapes.

Copy these shapes or
design your own.

Create a dinosaur landscape.

Spots, dots, circles and lines...

Lots of mountains, cabins and trees are missing from this scene.

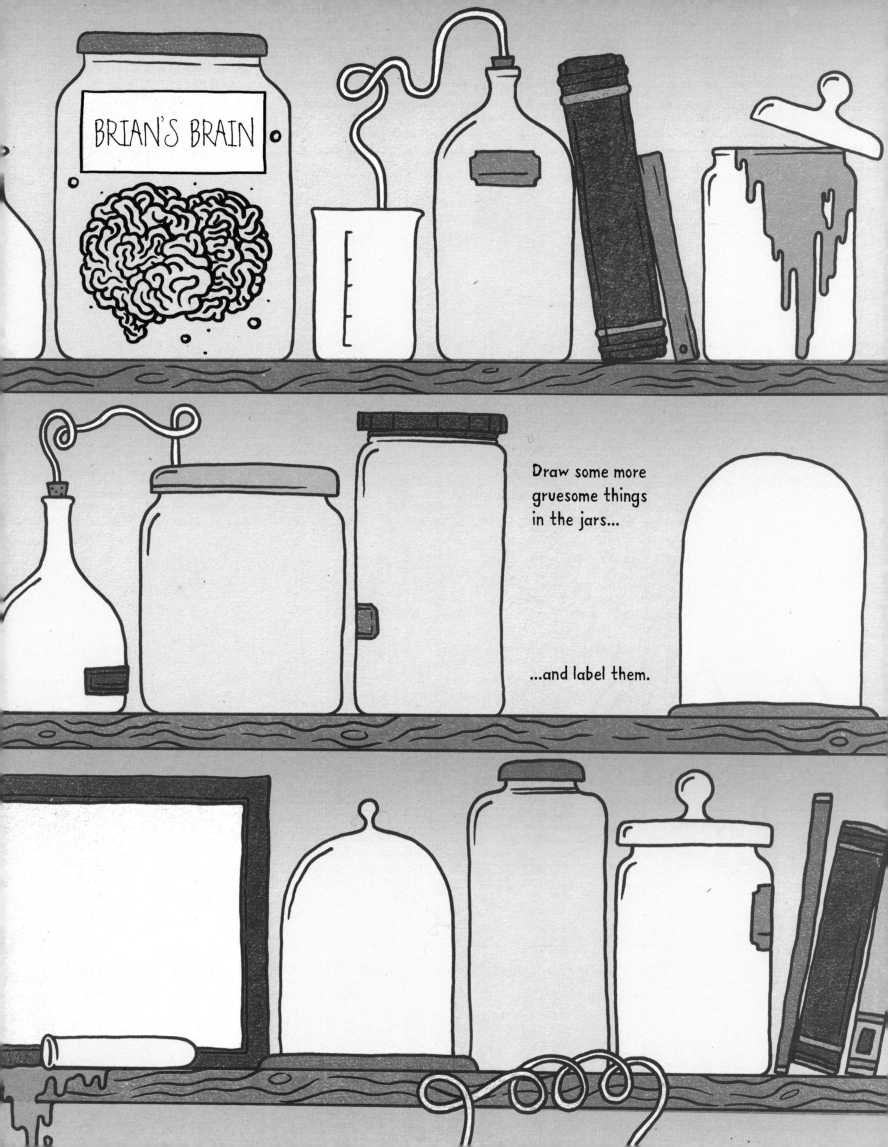

BRIAN'S BRAIN

Draw some more
gruesome things
in the jars...

...and label them.

Using a black pen, turn the shapes into skulls.

Doodle some greedy mice...

CHOMP

YUM YUM

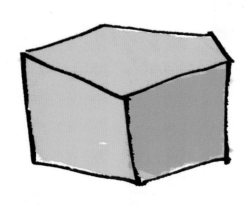

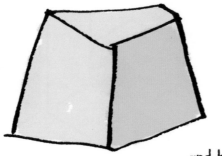

...and holes in the cheese.

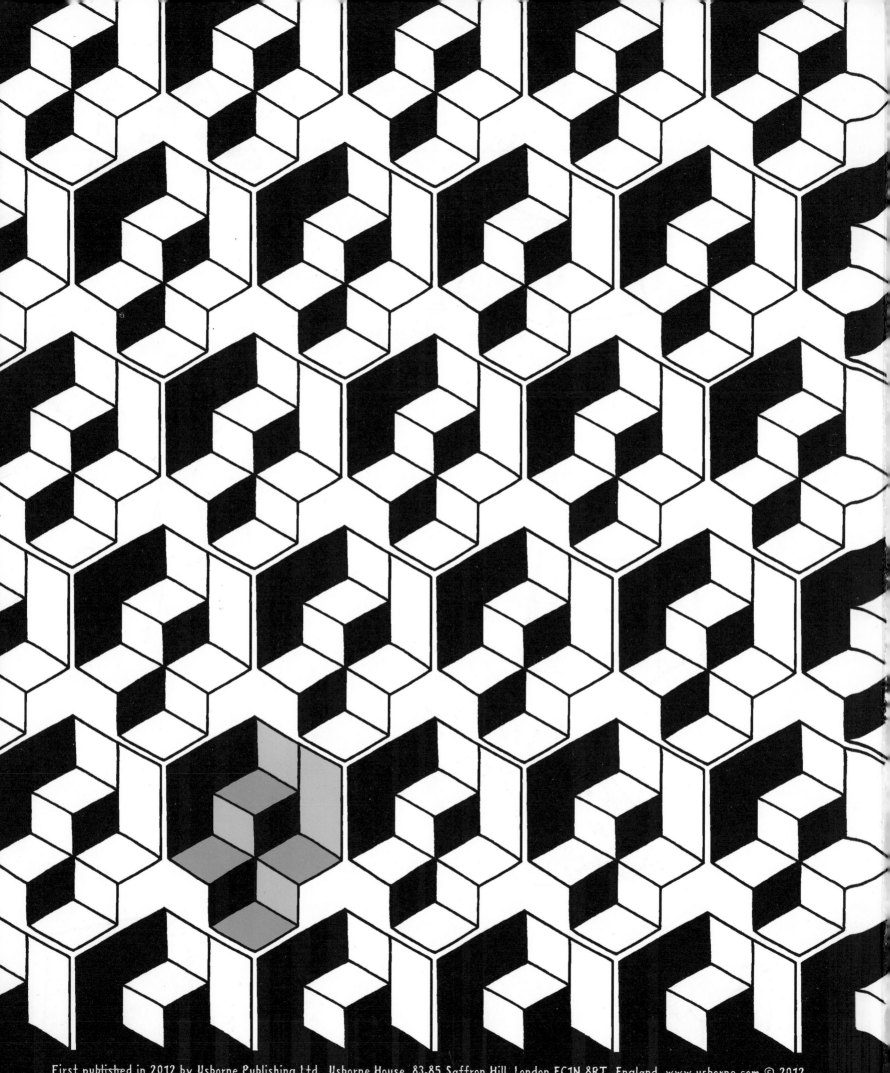